Tort Law

This is a brief synopsis of Tort Law. Pages formation is designed for notes. Torts Contrasted with crimes and contracts.

Notes

(Use this space to record and retain important information)

Foot Notes:

Torts are civil wrong s. Some wrongs can be both Torts and Crimes

Notes:

(Use this space to record and retain important information)

Foot Notes:

The Law punish the wrongdoer on behalf of society.

Notes:

(Use this space to record and retain important information)

Foot Notes:

Tort Law can be contrasted with contract law a major part of civil law.

Notes;

(Use this space to record and retain important information)

Foot Notes:

Categories of Tort

    (1) Intentional torts
    (2) Negligence
    (3) Strict Liability

(Use this space to record and retain important information)

Foot Notes:

Intentional Torts

(1) An act by the defendant
(2) With intent to cause a harmful offensive or touching
(3) A harmful or offensive touching occurs
(4) The act causes the harmful or offensive touching

These are the four elements to Tort

Notes:

(Use this space to record and retain important in formation)

Foot Notes:

Some acts are deemed intentional as a matter of policy.

Notes:

(Use this space to record and retain important information)

Foot Notes:

Common intentional torts

(1) Battery

(2) Assault

(3)Intentional or emotional distress

(4) False imprisonment

(Use this space to record and retain important information)

Foot Notes:

Trespass to land

Conversion

Notes:

(use this space to record and retain important information)

Foot Notes:

Defenses Against intentional Torts Claims

A defendant may escape liability by showing a valid defense.

(Use this space to record and retain important information)

Foot Notes:

Torts of Negligence

General

There is a vast variety of torts

Notes:

(Use this space to record and retain important information)

Foot Notes:

Paralegals need to be knowledgeable about negligence

Notes:

(Use this space to record and retain important information)

Foot Notes:

This category of Torts generates the greatest number of torts suites

Notes:

(Use this space to record and retain important information

Foot Notes:

and many of the largest monetary awards.

Notes:

(Use this space to record and retain important information)

Foot Notes:

Four elements of a Tort of Negligence:

Notes:

(Use this space to record and retain important information)

Foot Notes:

Duty measured by a standard of care

Breach of duty

Injury, and

Proximate Cause.

Notes:

(Use this space to record and retain important information)

Foot Notes:

Remember there is a special duty Breach:

Notes:

(Use this space to record and retain important information)

Foot Notes:

Of Breach determined by Res Ipsa Loquitur

Notes:

Notes:

(Use this space to record and retain important information)

Foot Notes:

Key Words;

Breach

Violated

Ordinance

Standard of care

Notes:

9 Use this space to record and retain important information)

Foot Notes:

Injury , amount of compensation

Notes:

Notes:

(Use this space to record and retain important information)

Foot Notes:

Proximate cause = Cause in fact + foreseeability

Notes:

(Use this space to record and retain important information)

Notes:

Foot Notes

Remember you have to have "Causation"

Notes:

Notes

(Use this space to record and retain important information)

Foot Notes:

Strict Liability:

Notes:

Notes;

(Use this space to record and retain important information

Foot Notes:

Vicarious Liability

Notes:

(use this space to record and retain important information)

Foot Notes:

A person can be held liable for another's torts

Notes:

Notes:

(Use this space to record and retain important information)

Foot Notes:

Worker's Compensation

Notes:

Notes:

(Use this space to record and retain important information)

Foot Notes:

Products Liability

Notes:

Notes:

(Use this space to record and retain important information)

Notes:

Foot Notes;

Defamation damaging of another's reputation

Notes:

Notes:

(Use this space to record and retain important information)

Foot Notes:

Invasion of Privacy

Notes:

Notes:

(Use this space to record and retain important information)

Foot Notes

Proof remember is a Tort action

Notes:

Notes:

(Use this space to record and retain important information)

Foot Notes:

TORT IMMUNITIES

A. Governments
B. Public officers
C. Charitable organization
D. Minor children
E. Insane person

NOTES:

(Use this space to record and retain important information)

Foot Notes: